Trail of Tears

A Captivating Guide to the Forced Removals of Cherokee, Muscogee Creek, Seminole, Chickasaw, and Choctaw nations

© Copyright 2018

All rights Reserved. No part of this book may be reproduced in any form without permission in writing from the author. Reviewers may quote brief passages in reviews.

Disclaimer: No part of this publication may be reproduced or transmitted in any form or by any means, mechanical or electronic, including photocopying or recording, or by any information storage and retrieval system, or transmitted by email without permission in writing from the publisher.

While all attempts have been made to verify the information provided in this publication, neither the author nor the publisher assumes any responsibility for errors, omissions or contrary interpretations of the subject matter herein.

This book is for entertainment purposes only. The views expressed are those of the author alone, and should not be taken as expert instruction or commands. The reader is responsible for his or her own actions.

Adherence to all applicable laws and regulations, including international, federal, state and local laws governing professional licensing, business practices, advertising and all other aspects of doing business in the US, Canada, UK or any other jurisdiction is the sole responsibility of the purchaser or reader.

Neither the author nor the publisher assumes any responsibility or liability whatsoever on the behalf of the purchaser or reader of these materials. Any perceived slight of any individual or organization is purely unintentional.

Free Bonus from Captivating History (Available for a Limited time)

Hi History Lovers!

Now you have a chance to join our exclusive history list so you can get your first history ebook for free as well as discounts and a potential to get more history books for free! Simply visit the link below to join.

Captivatinghistory.com/ebook

Also, make sure to follow us on:

Twitter: @Captivhistory

Facebook: Captivating History:@captivatinghistory

Contents

INTRODUCTION 1

CHAPTER 1 – THE EARLY RELATIONSHIP 3
    NATIVE AMERICAN LANDS 4
    AN UNEVEN EXCHANGE 5
    IMPACTS ON THE CHEROKEES AND OTHER NATIVE NATIONS 7

CHAPTER 2 – THE GROWTH OF MANIFEST DESTINY 10
    DEFINING MANIFEST DESTINY 11
    FORGETTING THEIR DEBTS 14
    RELIGION OVER REALITY 15

CHAPTER 3 – THE DISCOVERY OF GOLD AND THE INDIAN REMOVAL ACT 17
    THE GEORGIA GOLD RUSH 17
    A FEVERED INTEREST IN CLAIMING LAND 19
    THE INDIAN REMOVAL ACT 20
    THE REMOVAL OF THE CHOCTAW NATION 21
    SEMINOLE RESISTANCE 23

CHAPTER 4 – PEACEFUL PROTESTS AND A PUSH FOR RECOGNITION 25
    TAKING THEIR CASE TO COURT 25
    MAJOR RIDGE 27
    TREATY OF NEW ECHOTA 29

CHAPTER 5 – THE PEOPLE VERSUS THE PRESIDENT 31
Andrew Jackson 31
A Legacy of Racism and Manifest Destiny 34
A Quick Look at Changing Standards 36

CHAPTER 6 – THE MILITIA FORCE REMOVAL 38
1838 38
The Arrival of the Militia 39
The Small Group Who Escaped the Camps 40
The Drought and US Indifference 41
Ross's Plan to Minimize Casualties 43

CHAPTER 7 – THE TRAIL OF TEARS 45
The Late Departure 45
Taking Their History 46
Assassinations Following the Arrival in the New Lands 47

CHAPTER 8 – STORIES OF PAIN, LOSS, AND LOVE 50
The Indian-Pioneer Story Collection 50
Escaping the US Military 51
The Experience Along the Trail 51
An Early Departure 52
A Tale of Loss on the River 53
The Tale of a Muskogee 53
A Harsh Lesson 55
The Son of John Ridge 55

CHAPTER 9 – MAKING A NEW HOME 57
The World Rebuilt and the Second Betrayal by the US Government 57
The Cherokee Rose and a Beginning 59

CONCLUSION 61
Images of the Main Characters in this Book 64

HERE'S ANOTHER BOOK BY CAPTIVATING HISTORY THAT YOU MIGHT LIKE 67

FREE BONUS FROM CAPTIVATING HISTORY (AVAILABLE FOR A LIMITED TIME) 68

BIBLIOGRAPHY 69

Introduction

One of the darkest and cruelest chapters in the history of the United States occurred when the nation's young government decided to remove the native peoples from their lands in the name of profit. Having helped settlers for hundreds of years, five Native American tribes found it increasingly more difficult to relate to and trust the country that had once acted as their allies. The native peoples had fought alongside the Americans to gain freedom from the Kingdom of Great Britain, the nation that the colonists deemed oppressive and unfair. The native peoples acted as benefactors and teachers, helping the colonists to gain an advantage against an army that was far superior to the small forces that the colonists could muster. The new country owed a lot of its existence to the native peoples, yet the settlers, who were of European descent, did not see it that way.

Over the nearly half a century that followed the American Revolution, the actions and assistance of the native people were largely forgotten as the citizens of the new nation forgot their debt when the land of the native peoples proved to have something of value. Instead of respecting treaties, agreements, and morals, the Americans decided that they were the superior people, and quickly justified their invasion into territory that had been promised to the natives.

Tensions had been building for years as European settlers increasingly demanded more lands – lands that had been used by the natives for centuries. Many reasons were given, but the truth was that gold had been discovered, and there was the potential for Americans to profit by stealing the land from the natives. Perhaps fearing retribution for the theft, but largely through religious justification of genocide, they decided to evict the natives from their land.

There were some Americans who were outraged by the actions of the government and the President, but Congress ignored the outrage, treaties, promises, and what was right in the name of enriching a few more Americans. The cruelty exhibited by the young government by removing people from their land was matched only by the cruelty and indifference many Americans felt about the hardships and misery that the native peoples suffered when they were forced to march a long way to the resettlement locations. Ultimately, it was one of the most horrific and least discussed events in the country's history. Most people are aware that it happened, but the pain, suffering, illegality, and immoral nature of the activity is waved aside as being too far back in the history to be relevant. It is an ordeal that the native peoples never fully recovered from, especially as the country continued to push them further and further from their homes as white settlers were always prioritized over the very people who ensured that the earliest colonists were not killed by the harsh land that the settlers had adopted as their home.

Chapter 1 – The Early Relationship

The relationship between the native peoples in the United States and the European settlers was initially friendly. Once the settlers were able to achieve some level of security, they began to spread and take the land that they wanted based on the idea that they were the superior race. This was decided despite the fact that they only survived those first few years because of the natives who not only helped them but also taught them how to work with the land where the settlers decided to stay.

The approach that the indigenous people took to dealing with the settlers was usually one of a teacher, and despite their reputation as savages today, the natives were largely a peaceful people who were willing to let others live as they saw fit. This was seen as a weakness by the settlers, and over the centuries they increasingly wanted more of the land they saw. Some treaties and agreements were made, but over time, the settlers, then the Americans were more than happy to disregard or discard those promises under their claim that they were superior and could take what they wanted. Sometimes their claims were on religious grounds, other times, they were more honest about the fact that they were greedy. The Trail of Tears began as a combination of both of these reasons.

Native American Lands

Of course, when it comes to talking about the native peoples, they should not really be considered as a whole, any more than a person would consider all of the settlers from Europe as a single group. Many nuances and histories are not aptly displayed with such a broad, general statement. Some tribes were more violent and less tolerant, while others were openly willing to help. Some native nations were as complex and structured as any nation in Europe at the time.

The growth and spread of colonists had been of concern to the natives by the end of the British reign of the colonies. The *Proclamation of 1763* was meant to assure that the indigenous people would not lose everything to the colonists. The proclamation specified the area between the Mississippi River and the Appalachian Mountains as native lands that the colonists could not take. Once the colonists revolted against England and won the Revolutionary War, there was no guarantee that they would honor the proclamation, and in time they would prove as dishonorable as some natives had feared. Not only did the Americans fail to honor the proclamation, they repeatedly broke their own peace treaties and promises to the natives. Despite the area between the Mississippi River and the Appalachian Mountains being designated as strictly indigenous land, settlers soon started moving into it, even before the colonists revolted against Great Britain. It proved early on that the natives were never safe from the European settlers who wanted their own land and felt entitled to it, no matter what promises the governments made the natives.

Despite the string of broken promises, the natives were generally the more peaceful of the two cultures. Some tribes and Indian nations did fight back early on as the settlers pressed further into their area. The reasons for these attacks from the natives can be likened to homeowners today who feel justified in attacking people who break into their home. American history often teaches this resistance displayed by the natives in a way that makes it appear like the native peoples were in the wrong which can perpetuate the impression that what the settlers did was justified even though they did not stick to the agreements.

Before 1830, Native American lands still covered large swaths of the Southeast: Georgia, Tennessee, Alabama, North Carolina, and Florida. It is estimated that there were approximately 125,000 natives of many different native nations living in the area that came to be highly coveted by Americans following the discovery of gold. The nations included Cherokee, Creek, Chickasaw, Choctaw, and Seminoles, and all of them would be grouped together as a single type targeted for removal. All of this area was within the land that was promised to be reserved for the native nations based on the *Proclamation of 1763*.

An Uneven Exchange

Long before the Trail of Tears, there was an uneven exchange between the Europeans and native peoples. As is apparent by several failed attempts to colonize the country, such as the lost settlement of Roanoke, without the help of the native people, Europeans simply were not equipped to survive in the land that they were invading. A vast majority of natives were compassionate and decided to help the settlers to survive in their new home. They taught Europeans what plants could survive, when to work the fields, and provided the tools necessary for the colonists to survive. They helped with hunting and provided workers to help build the shelters that were needed to make it through harsh winters. This was true all up and down the east coast, from what is now called New England all the way to the coast of Georgia. Essentially, settlers were like infants who required nurturing and care to survive, and most native tribes and nations were willing to help. Two products that Europeans came to demand from the colonies were introduced to them by the natives: tobacco and chocolate. It can be argued that the first was more of a curse than a blessing, but it has made many Americans wealthy and continues to be a profitable industry today. When consumed in moderation, there are actually some health benefits to chocolate, although it was considerably healthier before Europeans turned it into a junk food.

The contributions that the Europeans made to the relationship were small by comparison. They did bring horses to the American continents, an animal that had originated in the Americas, spread around the world, then died out on the American continents about 11,000 years ago. The other primary contribution was the use of guns, a way of more effectively killing other people and animals and that required less skill and effort. Finally, they were accustomed to sturdier quarters than traditional native peoples' homes, at least on the east coast. They brought diseases and a religion that could be used to justify some of the worst atrocities in western civilization. Settlers relied on the natives, but still looked down on them as savage and inferior.

It is certainly true that not all colonists and, later, Americans took this view. Benjamin Franklin and George Washington were in awe of some of the political prowess and peace between the tribes that the natives were able to cultivate during contentious times. There were some that looked at the natives as a people to be imitated, at least in part, and many who preferred a peaceful coexistence with them.

The US in the 1830s has many similarities to Germany in the 1930s. Both nations had people who initially opposed and pushed back against the government when it obviously started to act in a way that was blatantly wrong. Both Americans and Germans eventually accepted the new norm within the country as long as it did not affect them. In Germany, it became impossible to ignore the fact that the new order was not functional as the country attacked all of the surrounding nations and oppressed even its own citizens. The majority of the German population was against what was happening, and they learned to live in fear. This was not the case in the US though. By removing the natives from their land, there were almost only gains to be had for American citizens.

Impacts on the Cherokees and other Native Nations

A significantly under-theorized aspect of American History is the substantial impact Native Americans had on the founding of the United States. It is often mentioned that the beginnings of the United States was formed with an eye on the early Greek and Roman democracies. However, there are arguments to be made that many of the greatest influences did not come from any European civilizations (either ancient or current), but from the admiration that the nation's founders had for the governance set up by the native peoples. Many parts of the *Constitution* were based on the founding fathers' interest and awe for the Iroquois Confederacy. Both Benjamin Franklin and George Washington were known to be great admirers of the Six

Nations of the Iroquois Confederacy because they were able to keep peace and work together, despite having separate interests.

The irony is that the reverence and admiration given to the native people were ignored as soon as it was inconvenient for the Americans in terms of getting what they wanted. It is a possibility that history was rewritten to pretend that the inspiration was derived from European cultures and not from the native peoples, clearing the way to pretend that Americans had a right to anything they wanted and owed little to nothing to those who had always lived on the land.

The Cherokee Nation occupied a large swath of the area where profiteers and prospectors thought they could find gold. When it came to fighting, the Cherokees were accustomed to peaceful means of settling arguments, so their first recourse was to approach the US government, and then the courts. They continually fought to be allowed to remain on their lands through peaceful means, proving that they were not the savages that the profiteers and prospectors continually tried to portray them as being. Ultimately, it did not help them because the rulings in their favor were ignored. As was proven with African Americans, the laws of the country did not apply to those who weren't of European descent. This was perhaps one of the worst miscarriages of justice as the courts frequently found in favor of natives based on agreements and treaties, but the politicians regularly found ways around this, with the Trail of Tears being one of the cruelest and unconscionable events in the country's history.

One of the major facilitators behind the trail of tears was Andrew Jackson. When he was sworn into office as president, he claimed to want to treat the natives in a way that was fair and just. In his first inaugural address, Jackson said that he wanted "to observe toward the Indian tribes within our limits a just and liberal policy, and to give that humane and considerate attention to their rights and their wants which is consistent with the habits of our Government and the feelings of our people." His words had been suspect at the time of his inauguration, but it had been seen as a hopeful sign that the Americans would honor the numerous agreements and treaties. Unfortunately, he quickly proved to be far less trustworthy than any of the presidents who preceded him. Before a year and a half had passed, the man completely changed his stance, backing the movement to remove the native peoples from their own land and forcing them to leave at a time that was more likely to kill them. His claims to want to be fair and just only went so far as profit. Once it became profitable to remove the native tribes forcibly, Jackson proved that he was not a man of his word.

Chapter 2 – The Growth of Manifest Destiny

One of the problems that is still obvious in the US today is that religion is sometimes used as a crux to justify the ends of questionable, immoral, or horrific actions. What happened in North America was not the first instance of Christianity being used as a reason to oppress an entire people. The conquistadors had already been far more barbaric as they slaughtered entire native nations in South and Central America. The Spanish Inquisition, and the Crusaders before that had already proven that Christianity was far removed from the teachings of Christ. The Jesus who had reprimanded a friend for harming a soldier when the soldiers had come to arrest him was no longer the prominent ideal. Instead, Christianity had been turned into a religion that somehow excused the use of theft, murder, and genocide.

Some of the settlers left Europe so they could practice religion as they saw fit. They would then turn around and force their religion on others, whether in their communities or against the natives. The Salem Witch Trials occurred in 1692, and it was largely used to oppress women who were becoming more outspoken in their new home. By the time the populace turned against the trials, 19 people had been hanged. After murdering 19 of the roughly 150 people accused of witchcraft, the court apologized and annulled the guilty verdicts, but the damage had already been done. Sadly, this blind religious zeal was not the first time when Christianity was used against people without just cause. The difference between the Salem Witch Trials and the Trail of Tears is that the courts would eventually admit that the actions were wrong, and admission of wrongdoing happened the same year that the accused witches were murdered. The US government has only offered tepid apologies that minimize the country's role in the cruel conditions and theft of the native's land. Little to nothing has been done to acknowledge the significant breach of the founding principles that were supposed to keep church and state separate. Manifest Destiny is part of the justification that was used to steal the lands.

Defining Manifest Destiny

The theft of native lands was not the first-time Christianity was used for less than noble causes in North America. It should be noted that the relationship between the British settlers and the indigenous population was generally positive. Unlike the conquistadors, the settlers were trying to make a home, so it was in their best interest to work peacefully with the natives. The terrain was less kind, and several settlements died off in the early days because the colonists simply were not able to adjust to the harsher life they found in North America. These were people who had never had to build their homes from nothing, so they were not prepared for all of the hard manual labor that was required to establish their new homes. During the early days, the natives were seen as a bridge between the settlers' old lives and the potential for something better on a new continent. The natives were seen as noble savages. Many of the settlers tried to convert the natives. Some of the settlers simply lived and let live.

Although there was always some level of contention between the Europeans and native peoples, for a long time the relationship was relatively peaceful. There were some colonists who believed that the natives were barbaric and should be killed. Just as there were some tribes and nations who were always hostile to the newcomers. However, most tribes and colonists saw the benefit of a symbiotic relationship, even though the colonists had far more to gain from the relationship than the natives.

This began to change as the settlers became more comfortable in their new home. They looked around and saw that the lands the natives occupied was better, primarily because it was land that had been worked for a long time and the natives knew where the best places to grow crops were. Because most of the native peoples on the east coast of North America were settled, and not nomadic, they knew the areas that got the best rainfall, and the locations that were ideal for fishing and living. They had established places to bury their dead, and all of this was established long before the settlers arrived. Many of the tribes, like the Iroquois and Cherokee, had complex governments and legal systems that kept the peace in ways the settlers lacked in the early days, as seen by the Salem Witch Trials.

Slavery was not a new concept to the natives as they practiced it within their society. However, they were appalled by the way the colonists treated their slaves because the natives still viewed slaves as people. Slaves were typically people who were taken in battle or war, and they tended to earn places within the society or work closely with the families where the slaves were to serve. Some were used in ritual sacrifices as well, which the Europeans saw as barbaric. The irony was completely lost on the Europeans that the natives treated the majority of their slaves more like indentured servants, and the sacrifices were still far less barbaric than the way slave owners treated their slaves. Having seen how Europeans treated their slaves, many natives stopped selling their slaves to the colonists because they did not believe that the kind of treatment those slaves would have to endure was acceptable.

Still, the colonists and later the Americans saw themselves as being superior and pointed to the fact that the natives would barbarically sacrifice humans to their gods. It was not all tribes, in fact, far fewer tribes practiced human sacrifice than those that did. When a slave owner intentionally killed a slave, the colonists, and later the Americans, believed it was a justified killing, like the killing of cattle. The slave belonged to the slave owner, so the owner could decide to kill a slave since the slave was not considered to be human. Most colonial slave owners found it more difficult to justify killing a slave if the slave was a native because they recognized how much they were indebted to the natives.

When the population began to be constricted by the area, the Americans eyed the land that was already cultivated by the natives. Manifest Destiny was their answer to defend stealing that land from the very people who had helped them to thrive.

Manifest Destiny was not a term that was coined until 1845, but the idea had been around for a long time, it just did not have a name. As Americans decided they needed more land, they decided to put their belief that they were the superior race and religion into use to rationalize pushing the natives from their lands. The term is an American term that says that the Christian God has made the American people the rightful owners of the lands, even the lands that belonged to others, because Americans were the destined people. They needed to spread their religion, democracy, and capitalism as far as they could, no matter what the cost was to the indigenous peoples. The Louisiana Purchase was the beginning of the great push to spread the "American" way as far west as possible, ignoring the fact that the democracy was largely based on the nations of people that Americans were removing from the lands. It is also interesting to note that Manifest Destiny was also used to justify taking Texas from the Mexican people, a people largely descended from Spanish explorers.

Forgetting Their Debts

To validate taking the lands of the original owners, Americans had to ignore all that they owed to the native peoples. Manifest Destiny was one of the few ways they could find to justify such a heinous act, claiming that it was their god's will to take the land, so it was out of their hands. The truth was definitely not an acceptable rationalization; Americans wanted to gain the wealth the natives were ignoring in the form of gold and the rich lands that the natives had been working on for centuries.

This kind of moral justification requires distance from the period when the colonists relied on the natives to help them survive. Most of what the colonists did to survive was only possible because of what the indigenous tribes had taught them. It had been several centuries since the settlers had ceased to rely on the indigenous peoples, and tensions had been growing as a result. Americans no longer needed the help of the native peoples, so instead of viewing them as benevolent humans who could provide guidance and help, the neighbors became a barrier to American greed. This was a view of a smaller percentage of the population, the kind of people who were more likely to view anyone as less than human when those people became a barrier to ambition or greed. People like Andrew Jackson could excuse terrible actions in the name of self-promotion and profit. Capitalism was seen as a good, and it was often at odds with the action of "good Christians." This was why Manifest Destiny became a necessary piece of propaganda for Americans. They knew that their history and existence were closely tied to the natives, and they could not overlook the role their neighbors played in helping them get established. The problem was that they no longer needed the indigenous peoples to survive. They needed the indigenous peoples' land to grow richer. This focus began to blind them, and many Americans lost sight of the debt that they owed the natives because they were too enamored by the potential riches they could gain from forgetting that debt.

Religion over Reality

Ultimately, the Christian religion was one of the main crutches the US used to defend actions they knew were wrong. There were those who fought against what they knew was wrong, disagreeing that the actions were justified through Manifest Destiny. They condemned the actions of profiteers and prospectors, and later Congress, for ignoring the reality of what they were doing. But there was enough of the population who believed in the justification of their religion to ignore the reality of what was happening.

While it is almost certain that those who spearheaded the idea of Manifest Destiny, such as Andrew Jackson, knew that it was a lie, they persuaded many Americans of the validity of this flawed thinking. Native peoples were painted as being savage and barbarous, and it was only the people who lived near the indigenous peoples who knew that this idea as a complete fabrication. Many of the cruelest, most inhumane, and barbaric actions were perpetrated by Americans, particularly slave owners. Again, their actions were justified because they were Christian. It was almost as though Americans felt that being Christian was the same as having a blank check to commit atrocities without being accountable for them.

Anyone who was not of European descent was seen as lesser, or subhuman, so Americans had a right to treat them as less than human. It is a really dark chapter of the nation's history, and it was based on a religion that was originally founded on pacifism. It is certainly a stain on the religion that it was used in such a way that was contrary to its founding principles and a tragic mark on the young nation that they would so quickly ignore the relationship that had helped shaped their new nation.

Chapter 3 – The Discovery of Gold and the Indian Removal Act

By the early 1800s, tensions had been growing between the natives and the young United States, but there was no real push to remove the natives from their lands because there was still much territory to explore, particularly after the Louisiana Purchase in 1803. Lewis and Clark were exploring the new territory, again relying on the natives to help them navigate the land and survive.

During the years following the American Revolution, the native nations had learned to work with the Americans in a way that was symbiotic without the Americans being completely reliant on them. The relationship was not perfect, but there were exchanges of ideas, and some of the native peoples adapted to the different cultures of the Europeans. The Cherokees even began to wear some of the same clothing and trade flourished between the two cultures. That all changed as soon as the Americans found something that the conquistadors had fervently sought in the early to mid-1700s: gold.

The Georgia Gold Rush

The news was not actually news to the native nations that lived in the Appalachian Mountains. They knew about the gold, but it was not the highly-desired metal to them as it was to the Americans. Perhaps they were aware of the European desire for gold as the European Americans were shocked by the discovery. Having seen the reaction of the Spanish Conquistadors, it is possible that the native peoples knew that the shiny metal blinded Europeans, making them incapable of thinking beyond selfish desires and greed. Or maybe the native peoples were so disinterested that it was immaterial that the gold was in the mountains. Whatever the reason for Americans not knowing about the gold, once the truth was discovered, it created a rift that would eventually destroy the relationship that was established when the settlers first arrived several hundred years earlier.

There are several stories about how the gold rush started, but it is certain that one of the first people to bring news of the fact that there was gold in the Appalachians was Benjamin Parks. On October 27, 1828, he found gold in what was Hall County, Georgia. Several other men discovered gold around the same time. With several people coming across the metal, prospectors and profiteers began to imagine finding the kind of quantities of gold that the conquistadors stole from the native people in South America. There was nowhere nearly the amount of metal in the Appalachian Mountains as was found in South America. The quantities found were not staggering enough to make many adventurers independently wealthy, let alone line their pockets like the conquistadors and Spanish monarchy had previously done.

Word of the discovery of gold did not spread quickly at first. As could be expected, those who knew of it were eager to find it on their own first, and so they kept the discovery to themselves as much as possible to reduce the competition. When the Georgia Journal published a story on two gold mines in the state, many other news outlets picked it up, and word spread like wildfire.

A Fevered Interest in Claiming Land

The problem with simply picking up and heading to find gold wasn't that it would be costly and dangerous; it was that the lands were promised to the natives. The gold was found in regions that were promised to be illegal for Europeans to own because the lands belonged to the natives. During the 1832 election, the people of Georgia voted for the candidate who favored letting citizens control the gold mines instead of the states. This meant that mines would have less regulation, making it easier to trespass on native lands with fewer repercussions from the Georgia government.

Most of the gold was on land that rightfully belonged to the Cherokee Nation. That meant that neither the state nor the citizens had any right to have mines on the land. To rectify this, the Georgia government seized the land that did not belong to them without any agreement with the native peoples.

A lottery allowed gold diggers to buy $10.00 worth of land in the Cherokee nation. The lottery also did not include a guarantee that the participants would find gold, so buying the land was an inherent risk. Between 1830 and 1837, the most gold was mined from the mountains, equaling nearly $2 million. Much of this ended up with the mint located in Philadelphia.

Few of the people who purchased land through the lottery got the gold that they sought. There were only a few fortunes made. The cost of the gold mine was severe for the native nations though. Because of American greed, the events were set in motion that would deny the indigenous peoples their lands based on pretenses.

The Indian Removal Act

The existence of gold in the Appalachians Mountains was not well-known in 1830, but there were plenty of landowners who were eager to lay claim to the fertile lands of the native tribes. Up until 1830, the US government had a habit of writing treaties to get what they wanted, constantly pushing native peoples off of the lands where they had lived for many centuries before the Europeans arrived. When the use of treaties failed because the native nations stopped agreeing to them, the US government turned to a far more underhanded method of justifying the push for native lands. The *Indian Removal Act of 1830* was the ultimate culmination of American greed and desire to force native nations from their lands without their consent.

Feeling that the land occupied by the natives rightfully belonged to Christians because of Manifest Destiny, Americans began to seek a means of ensuring they could get what they wanted. This was possible through a portion of the US Constitution that said that Congress could "regulate commerce with foreign nations, and among the several States, and with the Indian tribes." Although the founding fathers sought to ensure that the native peoples would be under "the protection of the United States of America, and of no other sovereign whosoever," Andrew Jackson was the first president who was not a founding father. Nor did he care about protecting the native peoples. His racism and bias against natives resulted in his using the Constitution to oppress and justify the removal of the natives, and he constantly encouraged Congress to follow his extreme, inhuman, and immoral desire to steal native lands.

Congress passed the *Indian Removal Act of 1830,* and it gave the president the ability to enact his own greedy desires. Jackson now had the process and tools he needed to start forcing tribes off of their lands by offering them land west of the Mississippi. According to the Act, the natives were supposed to be given monetary compensation to leave their lands, as well as the necessary materials to successfully and safely leave their lands. The ultimate lie was that the native people would remain under the protection and care of the US government as they moved, and after they settled. There was reason for native peoples to be suspicious of this new push to remove them from their lands, and some even began to fight back against the young nation that was starting to make it obvious that their only interest was in the land, and not in preserving or protecting the native peoples.

The Removal of the Choctaw Nation

Among the first native peoples to accept the toxic treaties spawned by the *Indian Removal Act* were the Choctaws. Living in what would later become Mississippi, the Choctaws were among the first to see that the world was changing. They were aware that the greed for their land was only going to become more fevered and desperate. In the hopes that the US would honor the promises of the Removal Act, the promise to provide help and monetary compensation, the Choctaw signed the Treaty of Dancing Rabbit Creek in 1830. The treaty gave them three years to leave their land.

Chief Mushulatubbee agreed to the removal and signed the treaty, but he was not the only chief. Nor was the Choctaw Nation a single entity. It was divided into three parts that reflected different values. The nation was more of an alliance where each part held different values and ideas, and not all of them agreed with Chief

Mushulatubbee and their removal. He represented the eastern division of the tribe, and he was concerned with the debt his people had incurred and the fact that deer and game became more scarce with the growing American population near their lands. His people had become fairly similar to the Americans in that they welcomed Christian missionaries into their lands. They owned slaves to work their lands, and they herded cattle in a way that was similar to the Americans. Chief Mushulatubbee hoped to gain more recognition as the Choctaw leader through the American government. While he supported removal, the chief also sought to keep many of the Choctaw traditions and beliefs. This was in large part because once the Choctaw owed money to Americans, the Americans had the hold over the nation needed to force them from their lands.

Once the treaty was signed, Americans were not willing to wait three years for the natives to leave their land, so they began to move into the still occupied lands. The winter of 1830 was brutal, but the Choctaws were forced to be the first to move along what would later be known as the Trail of Tears. Moving from their homes in lands that would become Alabama, Mississippi, and Louisiana, they relocated in below freezing temperatures to what would one day be Oklahoma. It is estimated that of the Choctaws who left during that year, 6,000 died.

Those who opted to remain were faced with an uncertain future as Americans were not willing to wait out the terms of the treaty before seizing the land. Following their relocation and substantial losses from their homes, the Choctaws ceased to be so welcoming to Americans on their lands, especially missionaries who would further erode their traditions.

Seminole Resistance

One of the next major native nations to be removed from their lands were the Seminoles. Living in Florida, the Seminoles had continued to control their lands through Spanish occupation of the area. Americans had been eyeing the land for a long time and were eager to take it from the Spanish occupants. No longer able to afford its once expansive empire, Spain ceded the territory to the US in 1821. Seeing the land as their own after having taken it from the Spanish, Americans did not have the same kind of relationship with the Seminoles that they had with many of the other tribes forced on the Trail of Tears.

Many Creeks had fled to Florida while it was still claimed by the Spanish following the bloody Creek War of 1813 and 1814. The Creeks joined the Seminoles, creating a nation of people who were unwilling to compromise with the Spanish, and even less willing to make any treaties with the US once it claimed to own the land.

In 1832, the Seminoles were told they needed to settle on the Creek Reservation established following the Creek removal. Tensions continued to mount as the Seminoles mostly refused to leave the lands that had belonged to them for centuries. At first, the resistance was relatively peaceful. For years, the Seminoles had been a problem to Americans because they refused not only to leave their lands, they also would not return slaves who had escaped to their lands (nor were they subject to the laws in the US that required Americans to return escaped slaves), and they largely refused to sell their livestock to the US government.

The resistance erupted into open fighting in 1835. Called the Second Seminole War, the Seminoles fought against the US for seven years and never signed a treaty or renounced their sovereignty. They were the only native peoples to refuse to do so. It was the only time the US had to use their young army, navy, and marines, and it still took them seven years to gain anything like a victory over the 5,000 Seminoles who occupied Florida. The Seminole people were rounded up and forced onto ships that transported them to New Orleans and up the Mississippi River until they reached Arkansas and traveled overland to the lands the US designated as theirs, far from their ancestral homes.

Chapter 4 – Peaceful Protests and a Push for Recognition

One of the greatest tragedies of the beginning of the removal was the way the event unfolded. Unlike the Choctaw and Seminole Nations, the Cherokee Nation took a peaceful, methodical approach to the *Indian Removal Act*, striving to prove that they were not barbarians or savages who could not understand how the young country worked. They used the court system that was so revered within the US to plead their case and to fight back against those who sought to throw them from their lands. Unfortunately, they had a much greater foe than people simply greedy for more lands. The Cherokee Nation also had to fight those who had no interest in long-term work and farming because they saw the Cherokee lands as a way to easy fortune because of the Georgia Gold Rush.

Taking Their Case to Court

Until the Georgia Gold Rush, the Cherokees were unique in their approach to staving off the encroachment of Americans on their lands. They fought, but not like the Seminoles. The Cherokee Nation took their claims to the US courts because they were aware of how bound the nation was by the rulings of their court systems. Even presidents were required to follow the laws set forth by the courts, and the Cherokees knew that they would strengthen their claims among the American people by using the court systems instead of shedding blood.

They also had a man who was only one-eighth Cherokee to help them navigate through the courts. John Ross was the prosperous owner of a trading post that helped elevate him in the eyes of both those in the tribe and in the US. He worked to negotiate for the Cherokee people in Washington, D.C. Ross knew the laws and was able to provide much of the argument needed to prove that the Cherokees were not the barbaric Indians that were often portrayed when Americans were talking about native peoples. The Cherokees were successful in protecting their people and their interests throughout much of the early 1800s.

Still, there was encroachment on their lands by settlers. The Cherokees would frequently take their grievances to the courts to fight the encroachment, something that the other tribes did not do. There had been several attempts before the *Indian Removal Act* to get the Cherokees to leave their lands, and they always answered back with a resounding no.

Over the years, the Cherokees had prospered and become more akin to the Americans in their approach to governing and lifestyle. They had project works and a courthouse. They even had a constitution of their own that they adopted in 1827.

The Georgia Gold Rush was the first real test of the new Cherokee Nation under their constitution. Ross would take the Cherokee fight to Washington, D.C., where he spent two years fighting the Georgia laws that had allowed for the lottery that gave away Cherokee lands to American citizens without Cherokee consent. Refusing to talk to Jackson about leaving their lands, he continued to work through the courts because Ross and the Cherokees had more trust in the courts than in a president who had a reputation for being bloody and merciless to native peoples.

In 1831, the courts seemed to rule against the Cherokee Nation. However, the chief justice added a few lines that gave the Cherokees hope: "the Indians are acknowledged to have an unquestionable...right to the lands they occupy." Ross saw his chance to continue the fight through the courts using American citizens so the court could not claim they did not have grounds to make a final determination. The case included missionaries who had refused to swear any allegiance to the state of Georgia and were arrested on Cherokee lands. In 1832, the court declared the arrests of those missionaries to be unconstitutional, saying that Georgia could not extend their laws into Cherokee land. The court further ruled that treaties were also meant to protect the native peoples from states that allowed their citizens to trespass on tribal lands. In a scathing addition, Chief Justice Marshall said that "Protection does not imply the destruction of the protected," which pointed out that the current removal of the native peoples was not a type of protection if it was against their wishes.

Major Ridge

Major Ridge was a Cherokee warrior who had fought along with Americans in several battles, and had gained respect among his people and the Americans who lived near the Cherokee Nation. In his early days when he first began fighting, Major Ridge had fought settlers, but over time he came to welcome them because the world was changing. His welcoming attitude toward settlers was at first frowned upon by the Cherokees, but in 1807, he gained a loyal following when he helped to kill chief Doublehead who had sold Cherokee hunting lands to some Americans for personal profit.

By 1813, he understood that the Americans did not see native tribes as separate entities unless a tribe provided evidence that they supported Americans. When the Red Sticks, warriors from the Creek Nation, began fighting with settlers, Ridge joined the Tennessee militia who fought them. He fought under the future president Andrew Jackson. It was actually a Cherokee warrior who saved Jackson's life, and it gained the Cherokee further recognition, except from the ungrateful Jackson himself. Not yet president, Jackson claimed lands from the Creek Nation following the loss of the Red Sticks to the militia. In that claim, he took lands that belonged to the Cherokees and not the Creeks. By 1816, the Cherokees had sent someone to Washington, D.C. to fight this theft of their land. In that delegation, both Ridge and Ross were included. This was when they learned just how ungrateful and untrustworthy Jackson was, giving them an advantage that other nations did not have. Their tactics worked, and most of the land was returned to them.

It was under Ridge that the Cherokees began to flourish and adapt their constitution. In 1828, Ross became the lead chief at only 38 years old, and Ridge was his counselor. While Ross fought for the Cherokee Nation's interest in Washington, D.C., Ridge stayed with the Cherokee Nation. With nothing decided by the courts, 500 Cherokee people decided to move and begin the trek west to avoid conflict with the restless and greedy settlers. Seeing the departure of so many people, Ridge became concerned that the Cherokees would lose their lands because they would be an easier target with fewer people on the lands.

As settlers continued to encroach on their lands, the Cherokees began to act within their boundaries. In 1830, they forcibly evicted settlers illegally squatting on their lands. This created greater tensions, and the worst elements in Washington, D.C. used this action – taken by the Cherokee against the illegal settlers on their land – to say that the Cherokees were not civilized.

It seemed that things were beginning to improve following the court ruling in 1832. The problem was that Jackson had become president, and his racism and ingratitude were as strong as they had been when the Cherokees had fought with him.

Having fought under Jackson, Ridge wanted to find another way to peace. By 1833, he had begun to consider removal as a viable option, and Ridge began recruiting others to his way of thinking. The Cherokee Nation started to fall apart as the paths that Ross and Ridge took began to diverge. The majority of the people were against removal to Oklahoma, and Andrew Ross, John Ross's brother, attempted to broker his own deal for some of the Cherokee people. Without support from all of the chiefs, any deal he made would not be considered valid by the Cherokee Nation.

Treaty of New Echota

By 1835, there was nearly no common ground between Ross and Ridge. The majority of the Cherokee Nation wanted Ross to continue the fight in Washington, D.C. to retain the rights to their lands, while a small portion sent Ridge to broker a treaty for removal. Knowing that Ridge and his Treaty Party were working to make a deal, Ross attempted to stall by saying that the Cherokees would leave their lands for $20 million. As he knew they would, the US government refused the deal and offered $5 million. Trying to buy time, Ross said he would take the figure back to the Cherokee people to see if it was a sum that would be accepted.

Impatient and manipulative, Jackson took an offer to Ridge while

Ross was gone. Meeting with Ridge in New Echota, Jackson had the same deal offered to the Treaty Party, and it required that all Cherokee lands east of the Mississippi would be deserted for American settlement. The Cherokees would only have two years to leave their ancestral lands. Ridge signed the treaty, knowing that it would mean his own death because he did not have the backing of a majority of the Cherokee people, yet he had just condemned them all to leaving the lands that were rightfully theirs. It did not matter to the American government, and even less to the immoral Jackson, that Ridge had neither the authority nor the right to sign the deal. They needed only a signature, and they now had it. This was the justification they needed for the removal of the people who had proved the most difficult to remove, not because of their military prowess, but because they had been as adept and civilized and so similar to the Americans. The Cherokees even had the majority support among Americans to be left alone. It was only the small minority and the president that they got elected into office that felt that way. They did not care about right or wrong, and they were willing to sacrifice lives to get what they wanted.

Learning of what had happened, Ross set out for Washington, D.C., to fight the treaty. He spent two years trying to keep his people on their lands, but he was unsuccessful. In 1838, the US sent troops to force the Cherokees from their lands, neither providing the financial assistance that was required, nor the materials that were promised by the *Indian Removal Act*. The method of the removal was beyond reprehensible, and it showed just how unethical the president Jackson was to the Cherokee considering a Cherokee warrior had saved his life years earlier.

Chapter 5 – The People Versus the President

The Cherokee people were not the only ones who felt that the US was going too far in removing them from their ancestral lands. There was a large percentage of American citizens who agreed that the Cherokees should be left alone. In a true democracy and a true republic, the people should have been heeded. Even the US Supreme Court ruled in favor of the Cherokees. The problem was that there was enough power behind the president, and Congress was corrupt enough that the will of the people could be ignored. It was not the first time, and clearly not the last in US history that power at the top levels of government was completely abused.

Andrew Jackson

When it comes to his legacy of genocide and grotesque views on other races, it is easy to condemn Andrew Jackson. However, throughout much of American history, the man has been revered as a person who fought for the common man.

His father died before Jackson was born. Raised by a single mother near the North and South Carolina borders, Jackson lived with extended family. His mother's hopes that her son would become a minister were dashed when he was still young and proved to be rude and violent. With a propensity for fighting and a love of cruel pranks, Jackson was not likely to be thought of as presidential material either. During the American Revolution, Jackson was only

13 years old, yet he fought for American independence. He was captured by the British. His refusal to do what he was told resulted in one officer slashing the young man with a sword. Jackson was not alone though, as his older brother was captured with him. Both contracted smallpox while they were British prisoners. The brothers were released, and Jackson's brother died soon after. Having lost her eldest son in 1799 and another to smallpox, Jackson's mother went to serve as a nurse, where she contracted cholera. Jackson was only 14 when his mother died.

Once the war was resolved, Jackson traveled around with no real purpose. He inherited some money following the death of his grandfather. It was only after the money was gone that he decided to finish school, then he became a school teacher. In 1784, he worked toward becoming an attorney, earning his license three years later. He was often characterized as charismatic and likable, but he retained many of his early flaws, such as the penchant for violence and a quick temper. He also enjoyed carousing with friends.

Jackson was appointed to the position of district prosecuting attorney in the western district that stretched from the Appalachian Mountains to the Mississippi River. Jackson continued in the position for several years. His inability to control his temper resulted in a quarrel and a duel in 1806. Charles Dickinson was attending a horse race and made a rude comment about Jackson's wife. Jackson challenged Dickinson to a duel. Jackson was shot in the chest, then returned fire, killing his opponent. This caused significant harm to his reputation. He withdrew from public life until 1812 when he turned to the one place where his temper would not be a hindrance: he went to war in 1812.

Jackson earned a stellar reputation as a general during the War of 1812. He helped to turn several battles into victories, gaining Florida for the US as part of their growing land claims. His military acumen was undeniable, though his morals and judgment were an entirely different matter. People were willing to overlook some of his worst flaws because he was likable and seemed like a self-made man. While this is not entirely true, he was able to turn a series of unfortunate events in his early life into a benefit as an adult.

During his life, he had come to believe many falsehoods about the native population, and Jackson was not a man of subtlety or deep understanding of humans. He believed in generalizations and made decisions based on a large paintbrush, harming thousands of people because of his inability to understand nuance. The reason why he was considered an American hero for so much of American history is that people have long been willing to overlook his obvious flaws because they saw themselves in Jackson. They wanted to believe that they too could find success after adversity, not realizing that Jackson was not the down and out man he was often portrayed as being.

The reason that it was easy for Americans to overlook those faults and call him a hero was because many of them did not suffer from his actions. He seemed to fight for the people, even though what he really fought for were the people who were like him, particularly prospectors. He did not mind people risking their futures based on false hope, such as the Georgia Gold Rush lottery, thinking that it was their fault for being swindled. There just were not enough American victims during the time of his leadership.

His real victims were the natives against whom he had a strong, unjustified hatred. Many had fought with the rebelling colonists against the British. Again, they fought with him in 1812. But

Jackson was not a man to look at facts to make a final decision, not when he could base his decisions on his feelings. The man owned more than 100 slaves when he died, and he treated them little better than cattle. He was a racist when racism was acceptable, but even still, some citizens had condemned his actions and his sweeping approach to dealing with the native peoples. Some were even willing to stick up for the people whom Jackson repeatedly wronged, although they were not in a position where they could cause him significant problems.

While Jackson clearly thought other races were inferior and that over time they would fall to white people with or without his assistance, he and his wife did adopt an orphan who was a native. The child died as a teenager, and did not see how his adoptive father ended up treating others who were like him.

He is also had authoritarian tendencies. While claiming to want to limit the federal government, he did a lot to strengthen it and completely ignored the decrees of both Congress and the courts. He brought people into positions of power based on their loyalty to him, not the nation. He believed that the federal government was always superior to state laws, and he put down some state laws that he did not agree with, far overreaching the powers of the executive branch. An entire party named The Whigs was made to stand up to him and his tyrannical tendencies. The Republican Party would later replace The Whigs.

A Legacy of Racism and Manifest Destiny

Jackson's hatred toward natives was certainly rooted in racism and a strongly held belief in Manifest Destiny. Whether or not he believed he was a man of the people, Jackson believed that white people were the rightful owners of all the land that had been acquired, and he did not like anyone telling him otherwise. When the Supreme Court ruled against him and for the Cherokee Nation, he said that the decision was stillborn, and he ignored it believing himself to be above the court's law. He was the accumulation of centuries of the worst in thinking against non-whites, and he made decisions based on those beliefs.

His blatant racism and continued push based on the idea that whites were the rightful owners of the land were beyond unacceptable to some notable figures of the time. Perhaps the most striking and famous American figures against Andrew Jackson and his treatment of the Cherokees was Davy Crockett. In his own words, Crockett decried the treatment of the Cherokees, "…at this time our Republican Government has dwindled almost into insignificancy, our [boasted] land of liberty have almost Bowed to the yoke of [*sic*] Bondage." He threatened to leave the country for the "wilds of Texas" if the vice president, Martin Van Buren, were to win the next election. He was actually a member of Congress when he expressed these views, and he did not wait for Van Buren to win before he left the US for Texas, where he famously died at the Alamo.

While many were pleased with the removal of natives who would fight against white expansion, the treatment of the Cherokee Nation was seen as a serious offense because the people were so similar to the Americans. There was a relatively large part of the population who had interacted with the natives, and the Cherokee people did not fit into the presented narrative about other native peoples. The fact that the Cherokee people were willing to work their way patiently through the American court system, even starting again when a new approach made it possible for them to present their case swayed many Americans to see the Cherokees as more similar than dissimilar. It was only the small fraction of those who were loyal either to Jackson or to their own ambition that pushed the Cherokees from their lands. While it could be argued that eventually they would have been forced from their lands, as Jackson constantly argued, given the favorable impression of them and the portrayal of them, it is possible that they may have found another way through the crisis if not for Jackson's blatant racism and hatred for all natives. Manifest Destiny and racism were the blinders that forced thousands of peaceful Cherokees from their lands, condemning thousands of them to death at the hands of an immoral leader who cared only about his own opinions and decrees.

A Quick Look at Changing Standards

Andrew Jackson was considered an exemplary leader for more than a century in the US. His willingness to make hard (and often illegal or unconstitutional) decisions earned him respect and admiration. It is perhaps unfair to judge the man based on today's standards because people did not think the same way modern Americans think. However, the number of people who disagreed with his decisions show that Jackson's beliefs were out of sync with many Americans of his time, but it was not a fight they wanted to fight. They believed they stood more to gain under him than they stood to lose. If the Cherokee people were pushed off their land, it was seen as unfortunate and regrettable, but ultimately, he would not be condemned for his actions until around the time of the Civil Rights Movement. It was only when the US began to really examine its abhorrent treatment of African Americans that it began to reflect on other glaring decisions in its history. It was only then that people started to re-evaluate their opinions and for the tide to turn against calling Andrew Jackson a hero and decry him as a tyrant and perpetrator of genocide.

To return to the comparison with Germany in the 1930s, it could be argued that Hitler had a different view of the world than Jackson. Hitler had lived through adversity, and at the time of his ascension to power, the German economy was in shambles with no hope for the future. For most of his time in power, the people were willing to overlook his atrocities, much as the Americans overlooked Jackson's atrocities. It wasn't that the German people or American citizens believed that what their leaders were doing was right, it was that the horrors did not directly affect them. This is true of many tyrants. What people are willing to put up with, and the kinds of atrocities that they are willing to overlook increases as they see improvements in their own lives.

There is some element of unfairness in applying modern morals to historical figures, but more often than not, people living at the same time as the historical figures noted the hypocrisy or wrongness as well. The problem was that it took time for the figures to be condemned for their actions. Thomas Jefferson was an incredibly vocal proponent to end slavery, yet he refused to end it on his own plantation. Alexander Hamilton was a philanderer who tried to hide it, knowing that it harmed him more than it helped him. People often know what they are doing is wrong, but they choose not to fix the problem. When those flaws result in the deaths of thousands of people, it is more than fair to apply moral standards from any time to their actions. It is vital to ensure that the same repugnant acts are not perpetrated again. The growing number of voices speaking out against the history behind Jackson and the US is a step in the right direction, even if it is far too late for the native peoples of the US.

Chapter 6 – The Militia Force Removal

The Cherokees did not see the treaty signed by Ridge as being valid because it was not agreed upon by the majority of the people. Ridge signed the treaty hoping that it would ensure that the Cherokees would be able to continue with some of their traditions in a new home, and because he hoped that they would be treated better. He did it knowing that it would mean his own death. His hopes were dashed as soon as the military arrived and showed no mercy and none of the promised money that the Cherokees were owed based on the treaty he had signed. Ross understood what would happen, and he acted to try to mitigate the devastation that occurred to his people. The two men continued to work for their people in the way they thought would save the most lives.

1838

One of the major problems with the treaty that Congress and the president used to justify Cherokee removal was that it was not a valid treaty to the majority of the Cherokee Nation. What Jackson had done would be similar to a foreign leader entering the US and deciding first to talk to the US president. Not getting the desired response, that foreign leader then went to the leader of the minority party in Congress and had a treaty signed with them. That treaty would not be valid by American standards because it was not agreed to by the person in power, and the majority of American citizens did not support it.

Jackson did not care that his treaty was invalid, or that his tactics, if used by any other foreign government against the US, would be considered treasonous on the part of the minority that signed the treaty. He got what he wanted, and he did not care how the removal was done. As soon as Congress ratified the invalid treaty by a single vote in 1838, Jackson's legacy was cemented. However, he was not the president when the two-year time limit was up; that dubious honor belonged to the new president Martin van Buren, the man Davy Crockett said would be even worse than Jackson. Van Buren was little more than a Jackson protégé, and he chose to perpetuate the illegal, immoral, and loathsome policies of his predecessor.

However, numerous people in power did not approve of the removal. Several members of Congress resigned in response to the initiation by van Buren to begin the removal. The General who was responsible for starting the removal resigned in protest as well, delaying the action and forcing van Buren to find someone willing to enact his illegal and underhanded method of undermining a foreign government that had done nothing wrong.

The Arrival of the Militia

Two years following the ratification of the illegal and invalid treaty, US troops arrived to start the removal process. In May, they began to round up the Cherokee people and placed roughly 16,000 Cherokees into a concentration camp until it was time to begin the trek to what is now Oklahoma. This was to be the new Cherokee land, a place where other native peoples had been sent years earlier.

All of the Cherokees who refused to leave or who tried to flee from the military were shot and killed on their own land by a young invading foreign power. The Cherokees who went peacefully where made to wait for at least a month in the concentration camp where Jackson and Congress failed to fulfill the promise of providing the necessary material for their health and travel. Many did not receive sufficient food and were malnourished when they finally started traveling on the trail. Some had contracted dysentery. Rape was an all too common occurrence as well. As the Cherokee people were forced out of their homes, white looters would enter the homes and take whatever the Cherokees could not collect in the few minutes they were given to get out of their homes.

At first, the Cherokees were kept in temporary locations, but over time they were forced to move to one of two concentration camps, one in Charleston, Tennessee, the other in Fort Payne, Alabama. General Scott, who was appointed to lead the military, claimed that his troops were sympathetic and cried during the removal, but far too many news outlets saw the crueler, more inhumane treatment now known to have occurred during the removal. Perhaps the men directly under Scott actually were upset, but too many of the troops believed the same lies and racist slants that Jackson had espoused. The results were actions that today would be considered atrocities, as would the entire forced removal of a people.

After the first month, the troops finally began to send some of the Cherokees on the trail to the new lands that were barren and nowhere near the equivalent of the quality of the Cherokee Nation's ancestral lands. Roughly 1,000 Cherokees left with the first group.

The Small Group Who Escaped the Camps

While the vast majority of the people (over 16,000) of the Cherokee Nation traveled along the Trail of Tears, roughly 1,000 people were able to escape the US military. They banded together and waited for the military to leave. They stayed in the states that are now North Carolina and Tennessee until it appeared to be safe. Some of the people were able to flee to lands in North Carolina where there was a treaty that said that the Cherokees in that state were entitled to their own lands without US encroachment. This was a place where the Cherokees could flee with some hope that their futures would not be entirely ruined by the ungrateful attitude that the Americans had adopted toward their people.

Founding their own place, this small group of Cherokees gained recognition from the government in 1866, and 1868, they formed their own tribal government. They still reside in Cherokee, North Carolina, and today are called the Eastern Band of Cherokee Indians. Some Cherokees left the lands they were forced to travel to in Oklahoma and returned to this place to live more closely to the way they had always lived prior to the US invasion. Roughly 12,500 Cherokees are living there today. It is a small comfort that not all of the Cherokee people were removed and that some were able to successfully outsmart the oppressive American government to find their own place in what had become a nation hostile to their people.

The Drought and US Indifference

Those who were rounded up were not nearly so lucky, and far too many died (an estimated 4,000) because of the indifference of the US government to the suffering of the people who had helped their ancestors to survive in North America. The US waited until the summer had hit to begin the move, a time that is notoriously hot and humid in the southeastern US. At the time, there was also a drought. Since the US used the promised money on making things easier for US settlers on Cherokee land instead of giving it to the Cherokees, as the invalid treaty had promised (further showing how little they cared about living up to their promises), the Cherokees did not have the supplies necessary to make the trip. The drought meant that there was not enough water for the first groups who left. Already malnourished and with some suffering from dysentery, the Cherokees began to die not too long after leaving their homes.

It is uncertain how many died in that first group or the two groups that left not too much later, but it was enough to force the military to abandon further plans to leave in the summer. Another concentration camp began in what is currently Chattanooga, Tennessee. Three means of transportation were used; train, boat, and wagon. Wagons were the most common means of transportation used. The boats that were to be used for the journey ran into problems because there was inadequate water for the boats to make their way up the river. The low water levels meant that boats became stranded along the Arkansas River when they were still over 100 miles from their destination. The land portion of the trek from the drought-stricken water proved to be even harsher, and the majority of the deaths occurred once the Cherokees were forced to leave the boats.

Instead of following in the wake of the three groups where many Cherokees died, the leader of the Cherokee Nation asked to wait until the fall to leave. This was granted on the condition that the Cherokees would not leave their concentration camps until they left. That meant that the Cherokees continued to suffer and began dying in the concentration camps where they waited without proper supplies or food. When they finally did leave, it was fall, and the majority of the Cherokees again suffered because the US government did not provide either the promised $5 million or the supplies required by the treaty. They would be traveling to a new, cold land without the clothing needed to stay warm. With US troops treating them like cattle and raping the women, the Cherokee people felt the full betrayal of the American government, and they placed considerable blame on Ridge for what happened. It was clear from early in the removal process that the US government was not going to follow through on their promises, and that added to the despondency and low morale that proved detrimental to thousands of the Cherokee people. There is no doubt that many felt that Ridge should feel the weight of the misery he had wrought.

Ross's Plan to Minimize Casualties

Chief Ross was able to lead his people over several different routes. After the route used over the summer proved to be too dangerous and less friendly to a people who were accustomed to a different approach to travel, Ross was able to work out a compromise for some of the people.

Ross had procured 645 wagons and 5,000 oxen and horses for the trip, a number not nearly adequate for moving over 10,000 people safely. However, since the American government had neither given the native peoples adequate time to collect their belongings and procure sufficient supplies, as the treaty promised, it was the best Ross could do for his people. He divided the tribe into 13 groups, hoping to improve the odds of survival. Three routes were established, but some people were able to take a less obvious route on their trek west. Roughly 1,000 Cherokees were in each group, a number that was meant to bolster morale so that the people did not feel alone. There were a few wagons provided for the trip, but most of the Cherokees were forced to walk to Oklahoma. Given that many young and older Cherokees could not make the trek on foot, they were given as much available space as possible on the wagons. Those who were not expected to make the trip overland were placed on a steamboat. The sickest Cherokees were placed in a group on their own, and the steamboat was to make their trip more manageable and increase their chance of survival. By this time, rains had helped to replenish some of the water levels of the Arkansas River.

There was one group that was not created or managed by Ross, and that was the one in which Ridge left the Cherokee lands. The group consisted primarily of those in his Treaty Party, people who would not be welcome among the other members of the tribe as they had allowed the Americans to pretend that the removal was legal. Johan Bell led this party. There were about 600 Cherokees who left with this group of people who were all but outcasts.

The path taken from Charleston, Tennessee, would take the Cherokee people through Nashville, and then through Kentucky, Illinois, Missouri, and Arkansas. Once they had passed through Arkansas, they would be in what the US designated as Indian Territory. The route, Benge's Route, was named after the Cherokee leader who managed the people who took this route to their new home, John Benge.

Ross helped the people prepare for the final departure from their miserable concentration camps. When the September 1 deadline arrived, the Cherokees were as ready as possible for the over 800 miles that many would have to travel on foot through a cold winter. Although Ross tried to prepare for the trip, there was no way for him to know about the winters in the lands that his people were not familiar with. The meager supplies he was able to prepare mitigated only a small portion of the needs, and the trip proved to be devastating.

Chapter 7 – The Trail of Tears

Although the first three groups had already made the trip, with a much larger percentage of the tribe losing their lives than anticipated, the worst was yet to come. Given inadequate time or resources to plan for the forced march properly, the Cherokees found themselves unprepared for a winter that was much worse than the winters they knew in their ancestral lands. By leaving the concentration camps in groups at staggered intervals, it was hoped that this would provide some help and support among the Cherokee people. It was one of the few bright spots of a terrible situation.

The Late Departure

The Cherokees had requested to be allowed to postpone their departure in part because of the drought. However, the miserable conditions coupled with the extreme heat had meant that disease had become a serious problem. Ross hoped the postponement would allow more of the sick Cherokees time to recover from their ailments. Having lived in an area with milder winters, it made more sense to allow the ailing Cherokees to convalesce and travel when the weather was kinder. There was no way that Ross could have known that the winter they were heading into would be far harsher than what his people were accustomed to experiencing. Instead of providing easier travel, groups began the more than 800-mile journey to their new home on less fertile and wilder lands.

Several routes could be taken, but most groups followed the primary route that Ross suggested. It is estimated that 12,000 Cherokee took this route. Groups left the camps over the course of the fall and into November. The last group left around early December. This group began their trek from Red Clay, Tennessee, but unlike many of the groups before them, they were not allowed to stop in white settlements along the way. With the Cherokee people plagued by the disease caused by the inadequate provisions and housing of the concentration camps, they were not welcome for fear they would spread the diseases that were a direct result of the US government's indifference and broken promises. The last group was forced to follow a route that would take them across the Berry's Ferry. Here, the white people took advantage of them, charging a full dollar per person, instead of the 12 cents charged to white travelers. Because the US government had not given them the promised $5 million by the illegal treaty, there was no reason for the same government to crack down on the blatant racism and opportunistic predation of the native people who were forced to take that particular path. It was simply further injury to a people who had already had so much wrong done to them.

The last group finally reached their new land in March of 1839, three months after they had been forced to bid farewell to their ancestral lands. They arrived to find other Cherokees already striving to turn the inhospitable land into something livable. Heavy rains, ice, and snow had significantly hindered them, but they were welcomed by those who had survived.

Taking Their History

Chief Ross arrived with the steamboat and a large portion of the sickest Cherokees who had managed to survive the trip. He had lost his wife, along with between 4,000 and 6,000 of his people on the trail. He had departed the concentration camps after all of the people who could walk or share space on the wagons and horses had left. He remained behind to help with the Cherokees who were very sick or injured and made sure they made it to the boat and were cared for on the journey. There were about 220 people in the last group that set out.

The experience led to the Cherokees to call the trail "Nu na da ul tsun yi," which roughly translates to "the place where they cried." While on the trail, the Cherokees had sung and attempted to begin commemorating the experience in their history. Their legends and myths were told, and new stories were added to those legends and myths by those who survived the harrowing journey from the place where they had once thought their people would remain in perpetuity. A missionary doctor traveled with the Cherokees on the tragic journey. She left records and stories of horror and hope. Based on her approximation, more than 4,000 Cherokees lost their lives from the time they were forced from their homes. This was close to a fourth of the entire population. Of an entire nation.

Assassinations Following the Arrival in the New Lands

The Treaty Party left separately, but they all were headed to the same place. Having personal knowledge about the president, Ridge had sought to find a way to gain some benefit in exchange for the land he felt his people were certain to lose anyway. He had hoped that by making a deal with the American government the Cherokees would find an easier process and kinder treatment than some of the other tribes had faced earlier. The results, although predictable, still were worse than what Ridge had expected. His gamble for peace ended up not only costing his people their land, but thousands lost their lives, and the government did not deliver any of what they had promised when Ridge had made the agreement. It was impossible to see the gamble as anything more than a failure, one he knew was fatal.

Ridge did reach the new lands with his group, including his son John Ridge and nephew Elias Boudinot who signed the treaty too. Though they arrived safely, they were not safe. In June of 1839, a small group of Cherokees killed him, his son, and his nephew. There have been some who speculated that the US government wanted to ensure that the Cherokees would have a more difficult time unifying in their new territory. Considering how many Cherokees died on the trail, it is more likely that it was not a plot by the government to discourage unification, but grieving Cherokees who blamed the entire series of events on Ridge. It was an outcome that Ridge knew was likely, but he had hoped the situation would end up better for his people if they had agreed to leave peacefully. It is difficult to say how he felt following the cruelty and savagery the Americans showed when laying claim to the lands he had agreed could be theirs.

Once Ross learned of Ridge's death, he was upset. Even though the men had long since ceased to agree on the proper path for their people, he still had a lot of respect for Ridge. While Ross certainly had not agreed with Ridge's actions, he could understand the desperation of his friend and the hope that it would work out for the best. In response to the news of Ridge's death, Ross said, "Once I saved Major Ridge at Red Clay, and would have done so again had I known of the plot." He mourned the loss of his friend and saw it as another setback for his people; not retribution for all that had happened. Despite his own personal loss because of Ridge's actions, he did not bear Ridge any grudge because he knew that the Cherokees could not be divided if they were to survive in their new territory. Even though many had little respect for Ridge after the forced removal, Ross still hoped to build a nation in their new home. It would have been easier to do with the man who had spent so many years fighting alongside him.

Chapter 8 – Stories of Pain, Loss, and Love

The stories from the Trail of Tears are mostly tragic, with many of them about saying their final farewells to loved ones, and sometimes entire families dying. The whole event is one long tragedy played out in stages over a number of years. However, Chief Ross sought to keep up their spirits and give his people hope in the new lands. Stories from the Trail of Tears were told to memorialize those who were lost and to reminisce about better times. There were even some tales about hope for what the future held.

The Indian-Pioneer Story Collection

Grant Foreman recorded an entire collection of stories as a way to remember what had happened and to provide a history of Indian families. The memories span a considerable period, about 100 years. Some were from written records soon after the experience in the 1830s. Other stories are told by the descendants who heard their parents discuss the trek and remember it from their childhood.

The stories cover memories by those who experienced it and the families who managed to stay behind because of ties to Americans that meant they had homes on American lands. Some tales are harrowing, others sorrowful, and occasionally ones that show the resilience of the natives forced from their lands by the greed of the new nation. Many of the stories are told in a way that is a matter of fact, relating more the truth of the experience instead of sensationalizing the stories. Still, the emotions and rawness of the reality are there, showing just how much the Indian people endured. All of the stories provide unique insights that humanize the reality of what happened.

Escaping the US Military

With only about 1,000 Cherokees finding a way to remain behind, it can seem as though all was lost with the arrival of the US military to start removing the Cherokees from their homes. However, Jobe Alexander had an interesting story about a small group that succeeded in escaping. Alexander was born after the Cherokee removal and settlement in Indian Territory. His father talked of a group, one of the last groups to be rounded up by the military. Unwilling to accept the removal, they revolted against the military. Their leader gave the signal to turn on the guards, and the Cherokees reacted by taking the guns from their captors and killing them before escaping into the mountains. The group was small, and since the majority of the Cherokee people were already gone, little was ever done to try to track down the small group who found freedom through fighting at the end.

The Experience Along the Trail

Lilian Anderson had grown up hearing the stories that her grandfather told of his experience on the Trail of Tears. He would talk about the primary food, roasted green corn and cornbread that was provided to them. Occasionally, the military who accompanied the Cherokees to ensure they continued to their new lands would kill a buffalo or other large game to provide some additional food. Water was scarce, and the Cherokees often had to go two or three days of their march without water. Their primary source of water was the streams and creeks they encountered over the hundreds of miles Along the way; her grandfather lost his family. He never knew if they got separated from the group, died, or if something else happened, but he traveled on with the caravan.

The trail was not an actual trail because there were no roads into the largely unexplored territory. The Cherokees who could walk would cut a path for the wagons and horses so that they were able to make better time during the heavy rains and colder temperatures. This often meant chopping up fallen logs and trees with axes.

When they arrived in Oklahoma, there was no housing for the people. Many stayed at Old Fort Wayne, a temporary fort that served as a shelter until homes could be constructed on the lands.

An Early Departure

As Susanna Adair Davis's story illustrates, not all Cherokees waited for the US government to remove them. Some had no confidence that the US government would fulfill their commitments, and they saw the writing on the wall long before Ridge signed the treaty that would be used to justify the unethical removal of the Cherokees. Susanna's husband's father was one such person. He and his wife were born in Georgia on ancestral lands, but they left in 1810 when the American government first began to make it clear that they wanted to take all of the native lands. In 1810, Cherokees were not under a deadline to move west, and they took their cattle and many goods. They were able to prepare properly and plan for the trip, increasing the odds of their survival. The father-in-law met his future wife as they trekked west with their livestock. He was driving his family's sheep, walking with them as they moved. She was riding a pony as she drove her family's sheep and cattle west. Sometimes the cattle would get mixed up, and this caused contention between the two families, particularly between the 16-year-old and his 11-year-old future wife. The experience ended up creating a bond between them and years later they would marry each other in their new home.

A Tale of Loss on the River

The Creeks were driven from their lands before the Cherokees were, and they followed their own path. During the move of the Muskogee-Creek Indians, there was a shipwreck on the Mississippi River that cost the lives of a large number of those traveling west. According to Lucy Dowson, a ship traveling with Muskogee-Creeks wrecked on the way up the river. The river was incredibly wide in some areas, so when the ship sank, a large number of Creeks perished because they were too far from the land. There were a few who survived by swimming to shore. Some of the Creeks were able to rescue others who could not swim. The bodies were collected as best as possible and were buried along the west banks. The Creeks were unwilling to leave for several days as they wanted to ensure a proper burial for all those who were lost.

The Tale of a Muskogee

Mary Hill related the tale of her people, the Muskogee tribe and their journey to new lands. Her grandmother told stories of what life was like before the trip, and then she would recount the harrowing tale of the terrible trip to the new territory.

The story began with the blessings of the land and the relative happiness of the Muskogee people. When rumors began to circulate that the Muskogees would be removed from their land, the members of the council tried to assuage those fears by visiting the homes of their people. Still, the rumors spread until one day the US government commanded the removal of the Muskogee people.

Although the rumors had been circulating, the command was sudden and unexpected.

Wagons began passing by the homes of the people, and it soon became clear what that meant. People were told to collect what they could and get into the wagons. Once the wagon left, they were never to see their homes or lands again.

The wagons took them to a temporary stockade where they encountered other members of the tribe from other places. It became even clearer that it was not just a small part of the population, but the entire Muskogee people who were to be removed. The people were penned into the makeshift stockade until the remaining people of the Muskogees were collected and brought to the stockade. Soon they were prepared to march. It began in silence as the people's hearts were heavy at the sudden and unexpected loss of their homes. Now they were on their way to a place that they did not know, having not been able to settle anything before being forced off of their lands. Like the Cherokees years later, many were too sick or feeble to make the trek, and they died on the way.

The horrors of the removal became more evident with every passing day as children woke as orphans and yet had to keep going. Parents lost their elderly parents one day, then their young children the next, yet they had to keep going. The silence and despair grew the further west the Muskogees went. Most of the time proper burials were not possible because the military was not willing to wait for the people to grieve for their losses.

There were a few men who were assigned the task of trying to raise the people's spirits, and keep the despair at bay. They would go around and try to lighten the heartache and take their thoughts away from the home they had to leave. They were to encourage where it was needed. Over time, women would begin to sing, reminding the tribe that though they had to leave their lands, they were still under the watchful eye of their god. That even through the trials, he was watching over them, and he would see them through the hardships.

A Harsh Lesson

Joanna Jones was warned about the US government and white settlers even as the Cherokees lived on the land promised them by that government. Her mother was born in Georgia and remembered how white people would enter their homes and start to take what they wanted while the Cherokees still lived there. They were rushed out of their homes and felt like cattle as they were thrown together with many others, often people who lived in entirely different regions. There were some who tried to take their valuables only to be told that they were not allowed to take those things because the Americans wanted them and would confiscate anything of value or interest.

Her grandmother provided the summation of the experience; "Some day you will be taxed out of your homes here just as we were there."

This was a harsh prediction of what was to come later as white settlers again began to want the land that the natives had cultivated since their forced move to the territories that were once not desired by Americans.

The Son of John Ridge

S.R. Lewis retold the tale of what happened to the Ridge family. Providing a brief genealogy of Major Ridge and his son, the story goes into their attempt to save their people and the repayment of death for what was perceived as a betrayal by the Cherokees.

The interesting part of the story is about John Rollins Ridge, the son of John Ridge and grandson of Major Ridge. When he returned to his home to see to his father's and grandfather's business, he noticed that a black stallion was gone. He searched and rode up to the home of David Kell, who told him that there was a black stallion nearby. Ridge ended up killing Kell, then fled to Missouri and joined a band of natives heading west to California. He did return to the old country once or twice, but he lived most of his life in California where he became a writer. He earned the name the "Poet of the Sierras of California."

Chapter 9 – Making a New Home

The Trail of Tears was only the beginning of a harsh life that the Cherokee Nation would have to adapt to following their forced removal by the US government from their homes. It was not easy to adjust to life in Oklahoma, and they did not have many material goods with which to begin their new lives. They lost one of their strongest leaders, Major Ridge, because of their need to punish someone for all they had lost, and that loss only weakened them further.

Chief Ross continued to provide the moral support that his people needed, acting as a stabilizing force as life seemed all but impossible. There was no point in time when he appeared to give up on his people.

The World Rebuilt and the Second Betrayal by the US Government

In August of 1839, the Cherokee people held an election, and John Ross easily won that election, becoming the first Principal Chief in the new lands. The nation soon selected Tahlequah, Oklahoma, as the city that would be its capital as it began to rebuild their lives far from the world that they knew. Today, Tahlequah is still their capital.

Ross remained in the position of the Cherokee's Principal Chief for nearly 30 years. The entire time, he fought to restore his people back to a state of normalcy and prosperity. He did not view his losses as insurmountable. Instead, he seemed to take an approach that was far more optimistic than the situation seemed to have deserved, showing how resilient he was and how determined he was to see the Cherokee Nation overcome what seemed like insurmountable problems.

Following the utter betrayal of the US government, as it went against the very principles for which it wanted to be known, the Cherokee Nation strived to return to the same structure that they had adopted when they became a nation. There were still parts of the US Constitution that applied to them, perhaps more so following all of the loss.

As soon as the people were more settled into their new lands, with homes and other structures built to provide for the basic needs, Ross began to work on grander designs. Over the years, he would ensure that schools were constructed so the children could hope to learn and grow so they could benefit in the same way he had from an education. It would provide the Cherokees with a way to fight in the future as they had been the closest of the natives to being left alone. It is even possible that the path forward would have been different if not for the Georgia Gold Rush. Ross also worked to have a Cherokee courthouse constructed in their new capital, giving them a system and order that were desperately needed. Returning their lives to something more familiar would help to prove to the Cherokees that they could overcome the challenges of starting a new life.

One of the other tasks that Ross pursued relentlessly was making the US government pay the promised amount of 5 million dollars. Too many lives had been lost, and the signer of the treaty had perished, yet the US had failed to provide the funds without any legal or moral basis to withhold the money. The government did make payments over time, but Ross would not let the issue drop until the government had fulfilled payment for the full amount they had promised. This was finally done in 1852.

Ross did not stop fighting for his people even as his health began to fail. One of the last fights he fought for his people was in 1866 when he was able to get the politicians in Washington, D.C., to sign a treaty that would ensure that any freed Cherokee slaves would be acknowledged as Cherokee citizens. This meant that freed slaves of Cherokee descent could join the Cherokee Nation following the end of the Civil War. This meant they would have a place to live instead of being left to fend for themselves in a nation that was divided and crippled. He died on this trip, passing away just two months before he would turn 76 years old.

The US government was not done harassing any of the native peoples though. Having promised that they would be left alone following their removal from their ancestral lands, the US government would again start forcing the natives onto specific, even harsher areas.

The Cherokee Rose and a Beginning

One legend that rose from the loss of life along the path came in the form of the Cherokee Rose. The Cherokee myth says that the mothers who had lost children along the trail were inconsolable, grieving for their children. In response to the apparently endless tears, the chiefs prayed for a sign that would help lift the women's spirits, a sign of hope for the bleak future that was ahead of them. The prayers asked for a sign to help the mothers push forward so they could continue caring for the children who were left in the uncertain future and pain. Once the prayer was heard, every tear cried by a mother that touched the ground would result in a rose blooming on the spot. The white of the rose represented the mothers' tears, and the gold at its center was the gold that had resulted in their removal from their lands. Each rose had seven leaves, one for each of the clans that made up the Cherokee Nation that were forced to leave. Today, Cherokee Roses thrive along the trail that the Cherokees took.

Nearly 150 years following the tragedy that was the removal of the native peoples from the land that was rightfully theirs, the US Congress finally took a step toward acknowledging the wrong that an earlier Congress had helped to perpetuate. The Trail of Tears became a National Historic Trail in 1987 as a way of remembering the pain, suffering, and loss of a people who had done nothing wrong, even using the US court systems to prove their rights to keep their own lands. Over the next 22 years, the recognized portions of the historic trail would double as more has been learned about the various routes used by the Cherokees and other tribes. No one native people were wronged, it was an atrocity committed against them all. Though a small step, it is at least the beginning of something that could eventually prove to be a benefit to the country, if the country continues to acknowledge and attempt to find a way to redress the wrongs. Had it been acknowledged earlier, the natives may not have had to suffer through the same problem when Americans decided to push further west across the lands after having taken all of the natives' ancestral lands without sating their greed.

Conclusion

The Trail of Tears began long before the Cherokees were driven from their ancestral land, long before the Creeks were forced to relocate, even before the Louisiana Purchase was made. The desire to take the fertile, already cultivated lands had always been a goal of the colonists once they had achieved stability and their own survival. The early thankfulness to the native peoples in the lands the Europeans began invading hundreds of years ago waned as their survival was assured. No longer concerned that they would not make it through the difficult weather and harsher living conditions compared to what they were accustomed to in Europe, their thoughts began to turn to greed. This was not a universal truth, and in the early days, many of the founding fathers expressed admiration for the native peoples. Not everyone viewed the people who had literally saved European settlers as barbaric savages. Many missionaries wanted to save them spiritually in return. Others sought to imitate the natives and their way of life. Still, others were happy to continue to live beside their benefactors as peaceful neighbors. However, in a country founded on the belief that "greed is good," the people who sought wealth and power soon took control of the colonies, and later the new country.

The very settlers that the natives helped to survive were like a Trojan horse. They arrived with the intention to find their own way and perpetuate their beliefs, whatever they were. Seeing in the natives a way of ensuring their survival while simultaneously looking down on the natives, the settlers established a pattern of making promises and then breaking them from the very early days of the colonies. Once they became their own nation, they became more like a parasite, continually looking for a new host for their own gains. Not all of them, but enough that they could achieve the genocide of entire native nations. The fact that so little was done by those who did not agree when they were in the majority proves that the inaction of good people does cause a net gain of ill.

Racism is an inherent part of the US, even being built into the Constitution to oppress African slaves and treat them as a class of sub-humans. Again, it was another area that caused a sharp divide within the fledgling country, and it was only after a long and bloody war that those of African descent would be allowed to live as free men, and even then they were not seen as equals.

By the time this war occurred, the US government had already perpetrated a heinous crime against the native peoples, something that actually ended up helping flame the hostilities between slave owners and abolitionists. As the country grappled with the problem of slavery, it was already too late to do the right thing for the native peoples.

The native peoples sought to make a new life on the lands where the US government forced them to live. Given the inferior quality of the land and the continual push westward that again encroached on the natives' assigned land, it became difficult to really establish a new life. Still, they tried. It is a debt and wrong that can never truly be repaid or redressed. By properly remembering the forced removal of natives and the forced slavery of Africans, and addressing the atrocities committed by the American government, there is at least the chance to learn from these experiences to ensure that nothing like it happens again. The darkest chapters in American history revolve around racism and a very flawed belief that any one kind of human can be superior to another.

Images of the Main Characters in this Book

John Ross, Cherokee chief. A portrait of him when he was 53 years old.

https://commons.wikimedia.org/wiki/File:John_Ross_High_Resolution.jpg

John Ross, Cherokee chief. A 19th century photograph taken near his death in 1866.

https://commons.wikimedia.org/wiki/File:John_Ross_of_the_Cherokee.jpg

Major Ridge, a Cherokee chief. Credit: DeGolyer Library, Southern Methodist University.

SMU Central University Libraries, No restrictions, via Wikimedia Commons https://commons.wikimedia.org/wiki/File:Major_Ridge._A_Cherokee_Chief._(15683664730).jpg

John Rollin Ridge, a Cherokee author, son of John Ridge and grandson of Major Ridge.

https://commons.wikimedia.org/wiki/File:John_Rollin_Ridge.jpg

Andrew Jackson, served as the seventh president of the United States from 1829 to 1837.

https://commons.wikimedia.org/wiki/File:Andrew_Jackson_Daguerrotype-crop.jpg

Here's another book by Captivating History that you might like

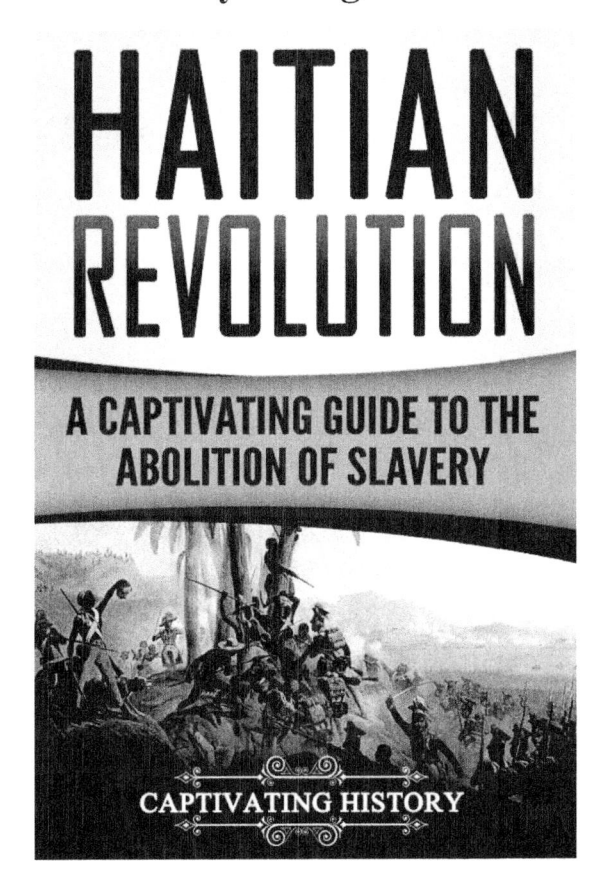

Free Bonus from Captivating History (Available for a Limited time)

Hi History Lovers!

Now you have a chance to join our exclusive history list so you can get your first history ebook for free as well as discounts and a potential to get more history books for free! Simply visit the link below to join.

Captivatinghistory.com/ebook

Also, make sure to follow us on:

Twitter: @Captivhistory

Facebook: Captivating History:@captivatinghistory

Bibliography

Andrew Jackson's Hermitage, Andrew Jackson Foundation, 2018
A Brief History of the Trail of Tears, Cherokee Nation, 2018
The Cherokees vs. Andrew Jackson, Brian Hicks, March 2011, Smithsonian Magazine
Cherokee Relations with US Government Before Removal, National Park Service, August 29, 2017
Cherokee Trail of Tears: About North Georgia, Golden Ink, 2018
The Cherokee & the Trail of Tears: History, Timeline, & Summary,
The Cherokee Trail of Tears – Timeline 1838-1839, Diane Siniard, Tuesday
Family Stories from the Trail of Tears, Montiero, Lorrie, American Native Press Archives and Sequoyah Research Center, 2018
Indian Removal and the Trail of Tears: Andrew Jackson's Policy of Indian Removal Led to the Notorious Trail of Tears, Robert McNamara, January 1, 2018, Thought Co.
Indian Treaties and Removal Act of 1830, Office of the Historian, Bureau of Public Affairs, 2018
Georgia Gold Rush, Golden Ink, 2018
Manifest Destiny - Facts & Summary, History.com, A&E Television Networks, LLC, 2018
Mushulatubbee and Choctaw Removal: Chiefs Confront a Changing World, Greg O'Brien, Mississippi Historical Society, 2017
Sacred Gifts, Profane Pleasures: A History of Tobacco and Chocolate in the Atlantic World, Marcy Norton, 2018, Cornell University Press
Salem Witch Trials, History.com, A&E Television Networks, LLC, 2018
Seminole Tribe of Florida - History, Indian Resistance and Removal, Seminole Tribe of Florida, 2018
The Surprising History of America's Wild Horses, Jay F. Kirkpatrick and Patricia M. Fazio, July 24, 2008, LiveScience
June 10, 2014, Native American Project,
Trail of Tears Timeline, Softschools.com 2018 Study.com 2018
Trail of Tears, History.com, A&E Television Networks, LLC, 2018
Trail of Tears, Elizabeth Prine Pauls, Encyclopaedia Britannica Inc, 2018
Trail of Tears: National Historic Trail: Stories, National Park Service, 2018
Trail of Tears National Historic Trail in Tennessee: Indian Removal in the Cherokee Nation, Toye E. Heape, Native History Association, 2017

Printed in Great Britain
by Amazon